Never T[illegible]

A Mature Student's Guide to Going to University

By Joanne M. Weselby

Print Edition

Contents

Introduction

The decision to go to University is a big deal, and as such, it can make even the surest of souls start to feel uncertain of themselves. Questions of "is this right for me?", "can I afford it?" and "will I fit in?" will understandably be buzzing around the heads of those planning to start their studies this autumn. However, for the mature students amongst those numbers, worries like these may be casting significantly bigger shadows right about now.

That's because attending University straight after taking A-Levels is often described as being part of "The Experience": a chance to fly the nest, to party, and to grow up a bit (or at least figure out how the washing machine works). Even if you're not set on a particular career path, it's almost *expected* that you'll go if you're the academic type. Plus, there's also a good chance that the Halls of Residence will be swimming with potential new BFFs, all filled with the same nervous excitement and looking to extend their social circles during the chaos of Freshers' Week.

However, choosing to go back to school after a considerable break is an entirely different prospect. It marks a change and/or progression of career or, at the very least, a monumental life adjustment. That places a great deal of pressure upon academic success, especially given the exacerbated tuition fees (which can span into tens of thousands of pounds) – once you've learnt the value of money, deciding to indebt yourself so heavily is not a decision you take lightly.

So, you might ask, why go back to school at all? It's a question I was asked many times, and one that I think it is very important to answer.

It's a way of challenging the unspoken assumption in our society that once we reach a certain age, we will have figured out what we want to do with our lives and will already be some way towards achieving that goal. For many people, that simply isn't the case: whether they've discovered that progress in their chosen field is limited without the right qualifications, or have decided to take their careers in an entirely new direction, the decision to go to University can be a conscious decision to advance their positions or change direction in their lives.

For me, the choice to begin studying for my Bachelor's Degree was prompted by my need to create something positive for myself. When I made the decision to take the plunge I was 25, struggling with my health and, despite possessing a decent set of A-Level qualifications, found myself unable to find a job even at minimum wage. I had officially hit rock bottom. Though University had always been a part of my overall life plan, I had decided to enter the workforce directly after college – thinking of it as little more than a gap year – and had spent several years moving around from job to job, organisation to organisation, trying to find my place in the world. I had worked in housing, tax, management, and customer service amongst other things, but never felt satisfied in what I was doing. Truth be told, I felt utterly lost. Entering the workforce had seemed like such a good idea all those years ago, but I had now realised that going back to school offered me the opportunity to test myself, to grow, to learn, and to become something more than I was currently.

Despite all that – or, perhaps, because of it – I must admit that I was extremely nervous about becoming a student again. I had always been an overachiever and prided myself on my ability to excel, but it had been a long time since I had completed a piece of coursework, sat an exam, or even so much as attended a class. Despite only being 8 or so years older than the other students enrolling that year, doubts had already begun to seep into my mind: I bandied around phrases like ‘too old’ and ‘past it’, wondering if my time had come and gone. I imagined turning up on the first day to stares, whispers and sniggers; to people wondering what on Earth I was doing there. I imagined being surrounded by whizz-kids who had the benefit of arriving fresh from their A-Level studies that would leave me standing in the dust, looking like an idiot. Worst of all, though, I imagined that once I got there I’d find out that I wasn’t as good as I thought I was, and I would let myself (and everyone that was rooting for me – my family, friends, and so on) down.

Four years on, these fears seem ludicrous: I am now the proud recipient of a first-class honours degree, and I even got a couple of academic prizes thrown in for good measure! I can say with all honesty that going back was the best decision I ever made. However, I have never forgotten just how scary it was taking those first few steps towards returning to University.

If you’re a mature student who’s feeling the same way, or you’re thinking about going back to school but haven’t made up your mind yet, then this book is meant for you! Enclosed within the following chapters are a few hints, tips and anecdotes intended to help you to make the most of both the social and academic elements of University life, and to let go of the fear that comes with deciding to go back to school.

Filling In Your Application

The first step in attaining your University degree is, of course, plucking up the courage to actually apply in the first place. Sounds simple, right? Well, not necessarily. There are many different decisions that need to be made before applying to study at a particular University – such as where to study, which course to apply for, and how to maximise your chances of being accepted – and this can potentially put off some people who find the whole process bewildering. With this in mind, this chapter will briefly consider the various choices that you will need to make when completing your application, and will also provide you with some advice about how to portray yourself in your UCAS personal statement.

The first (and most important) decision that you will ever make about your future is what, and where, you choose to study. Firstly, let's consider the 'what'. Choosing a subject can be difficult, especially if you don't have a particular career path already planned out and would be interested in pursuing several of your interests further. What you need to bear in mind is that, although you obviously want to choose something that will translate well in the employment world, you also need to think carefully about what topics you can handle studying in this much depth... the two don't necessarily correspond well. Let me give you an example: I love writing, and anything to do with it. Initially, I wondered whether I should include 'Journalism' in my list of possible options, given that this is probably the clearest route into a writing job after employment. However, studying Journalism is very different to studying English Literature – there is more focus given to other mediums of reporting, such as broadcasting, and a much tighter rein on what you can and cannot write about. I soon realised that if I studied Journalism, although I would get to write, I would also miss out on studying the things that really make me happy – books! Similarly, if I studied 'English Literature' without a creative writing element included, I would get to critique other people's books, but wouldn't get the opportunity to learn all the appropriate skills to be able to write one of my own. My point is this: there are a wide variety of choices for a reason. Make sure that you think carefully about all of the aspects of the courses that you apply for, and that you know from the outset which you'd rather be doing. Otherwise, you risk finding yourself halfway through your second year, wishing you'd chosen something else.

Now, let's consider study locations. As a mature student, choosing where to study can involve some difficult decisions. Unlike your average 18 year old, it is not necessarily possible for you to just drop everything and move to an entirely new location – you may have familial ties, work commitments, and/or other responsibilities that restrict your choices, or you might have to uproot more than just yourself in order to pursue your studies. Fortunately, for me, this decision was relatively simple: I decided almost immediately to study in Nottingham, rather than moving to a new city, because that meant that I could remain close to my friends and family, easily locate a part-time job to support myself during University, and continue living in the flat that I had grown very fond of. However, as with most major cities, Nottingham offers more than one option in regards to University choices… how, then, did I decide which institution I would rather attend?

As you've probably gathered from the application form, it's very important that you know your order of preference (that is, which course/institution is your first choice, second choice, and so on) before you even begin filling in the form. The reason for this is very simple: you get a maximum of 6 choices, which act as an insurance policy, just in case you don't get accepted onto your most preferred course. Let's say, for example, that I applied for three courses at Nottingham Trent University, and 3 courses at Nottingham University – making 6 in total. Say my first choice is the 'BA (Hons) English Literature and Creative Writing' at Nottingham Trent University. If I am accepted onto this course, all the other options become irrelevant. However, if I am *not* accepted onto this course, I still have 5 more chances left to get onto a course of my choosing.

One of the advantages of applying to UCAS as a mature student is that it's likely you are not waiting on A-Level examination results, meaning you will receive an 'Unconditional Offer' (i.e. unconditional acceptance onto your chosen course) if you are successful, as it will be based on qualifications and experience you already have. In contrast, anyone who has applied whilst still waiting for their results will only be able to attain a 'Conditional Offer' (i.e. acceptance onto the course, providing that sufficient grades are obtained) – something which makes the process a lot more uncertain.

However, there are still a considerable number of hoops that you'll need to jump through before you ever set foot on campus officially as a member of your chosen University's ranks. UCAS forms are infamous for their unnecessarily complicated nature. However, the accompanying guide can help you to find the unique institution and course codes you need, so you can complete your application relatively hassle-free as long as you read the instructions provided to you carefully. Student Finance applications can also be tricky if you're not sure what you're doing, but again, there's an excellent customer service support system in place that can assist you with any queries you may have about what to apply for and how to complete the forms. In this regard, the best advice I can give you is to start your application *as soon as possible*. Given the high volume of students applying every year, there can be considerable delays, and the last thing you need is to find yourself without confirmation and/or funding on the first day of term.

Most people agree that the most challenging aspect of the whole application process is not the multitude of forms or the coding systems, but instead relates to the completion of the Personal Statement. It can actually be quite difficult to write down all the reasons why your chosen institution should pick you over all the other applicants, even when you know in your heart that you deserve a place. My tip for writing an effective Personal Statement? Simple – imagine you're compiling your own obituary. I know it sounds weird (and really quite morbid), but you don't actually need to imagine that you're going to die – just what you would like people to say about you; how you would hope to be seen by those around you. Think about it…where else, other than when bereaved, are people so eloquent, open and honest about the way they perceive one another? This technique can help you to identify your best traits whilst putting all the discontentment you have about yourself aside. So, take a moment now to think about what those who know you best would say about you. What are your best traits? What are you good at? What are your hopes, your ambitions, your dreams? What is it that makes you so unique and special? Answering questions like these can really help you to establish the bare bones of what you're trying to say.

Don't be afraid to acknowledge the fact that you are a mature student when writing your Personal Statement – if anything, this fact gives you a clear advantage over other, younger applicants. You can make it clear in your statement that you have thought the decision through carefully and that, given your maturity, you will be more capable of retaining focus and determination throughout your course, despite any challenges you may face along the way. Remember: Universities *want* students who offer them diversity and experience and, as an older person, your viewpoint, priorities, and outside interests will likely be different to the average teenager. That makes you all the more desirable in the academic sense.

If you're struggling to find a theme or focus for your statement, it might help for you to start by explaining your reasons for wanting to go back to school in the first place. Often, this can reveal a great deal about who you are, why you feel this is the right time for you to study, and what is really important to you in your life. Perhaps you're determined to obtain a degree so as to provide more for your family, or maybe now that your children have grown up, you've decided it's time you did something for yourself. Whatever the reason, be proud to tell them who you are. There's no shame in blowing your own trumpet every once in a while, and I bet if you really thought about it, there are plenty of good things that could be said about you. It's time you started saying them!

Finally, make sure to thoroughly proofread your Personal Statement before submission. If you're not confident in this area, ask a family member or friend to check it for you. Don't just rely on the SpellChecker function offered by your word processing programme, as these often fail to flag up mistakes which *will* be noticed when your application is received and processed. A good method to use if you're doing your own proofreading is to read your statement aloud – this helps you to get the structure, pacing and grammatical markers within your sentences right, as well as making sure that everything that you've written makes sense.

Once your application has been completed, it's really just a waiting game. Don't worry if you don't receive a response within the first few weeks of applying – some Universities don't begin to make offers until the A-Level examination period gets underway (in June), so you might find that whilst you get a quick reply from some places, others don't respond at all for a few months. This doesn't mean that your application has not been successful – every institution does things a little differently. Plus, you can always contact UCAS directly to ensure your application has been correctly received if you're really worried – they'll be able to confirm that you have been put forward for all of your chosen courses.

Hopefully, this chapter will have given you a better idea of what to expect when applying to go to University. The remainder of the book will now focus on how to cope once you actually get there.

Getting to Grips with University Life

If you're still reading, that means you've made it through the initial stages and have obtained a place at University. Well done! However, once you've gotten your confirmation letter, you might find yourself worrying about actually *attending*. On your first day, for instance, it may feel like there is a neon sign hanging over your head, pointing out your existence – and your age – to all those in proximity. That's certainly how I felt. Despite being dressed inconspicuously (in jeans, a quirky t-shirt and a beanie – my standard attire), I was certain that at any moment, someone would expose my terrible secret: that, Gods forbid, I was quite a way from being 18. It was only when I realised that the youngsters surrounding me were feeling just as disorientated and bewildered as I was that I started to calm down a bit.

Truth is, everyone is far too wrapped up trying to get to their classes, find a good seat and locate the toilets, cafeteria and bar in the first few days to pay any attention to the people around them. They are all unsure of themselves and desperately trying not to say and/or do something stupid that they will be remembered for throughout their school career. They're new here, too, and for some people, that might present a challenge which they've as yet never faced – they might not be used to getting themselves to and from places, or having to take responsibility for organising themselves (I mean, we all know the old clichés about teenage boys using their mothers as alarm clocks, taxi services, cooks, cleaners, and all-round PAs). Therefore, the last thing on their minds will be the ages of the people around them!

When my age *was* eventually revealed – 3 days in, during an icebreaking session which included divulging personal details about ourselves, such as our dates of birth, in order to create our author profiles – I was pleasantly surprised by the reaction I received. After a brief moment of confusion, in which my assigned partner painstakingly counted out all 25 of the years that had passed since my birth year, thinking she had made some sort of mistake, I was informed that I could "easily pass for a teenager". The subject passed without further comment, and I was left to contemplate how much I had overestimated the importance of my age to my younger counterparts. So, what's the lesson here? Basically, you need to stop worrying about what your fellow students might or might not think of you, and instead let yourself soak up the experience of your first few days as a University student, for it will be unlike any other kind of study you have undertaken before.

The first thing you'll have to come to terms with as a University student is that you, and you alone, are responsible for your learning. Sure, you'll attend a few classes a week and your core reading will be instructed from a set list, but that only accounts for a small portion of the studying that you will actually undertake as part of your degree. Most of the information you learn at University will actually be sourced by your own explorative reading, research and investigation. For instance, you will often be asked to learn about something *before* it's discussed in class, meaning that it's up to you to figure out the concept, idea, or meaning of the text for yourself, rather than relying on your lecturers to explain it to you. Furthermore, you will be expected to make connections between different theories and viewpoints, as well as offering your *own* critical opinions to the mix, whenever you're given something new to study.

To make things even more complicated, in some subjects (like English Literature, for instance) there aren't necessarily 'right' and 'wrong' answers to the questions students are presented with: you will therefore have to analyse numerous different perspectives, and it will be left to you to decide which one you think is right (or to explain why you disagree with all of the critics' views). In order to do this, you have to change the way you approach and engage with the texts you've been given – this means no more passive reading and learning. Rather than being able to treat the contents of your textbooks as fact, you will be expected to constantly evaluate the authors' efforts, locate flaws in their arguments, and criticise their findings. Even in the more scientific disciplines, you will be expected to identify disproven data and summarise the limitations of the studies you encounter as a matter of course.

There is, in fact, a very good reason for this: your opinion is now considered to be as valid as those put forward by the authors of the books you're reading (Yes, really!). That's why you call your lecturers by their first names, rather than "Sir" or "Miss"… you're there as an academic in your own right. At first, this realisation can be scary, especially if it's been a long time since you undertook any kind of educational activity and are unsure where to start looking for the information you need. However, this also offers you a lot of freedom in terms of what you choose to study and how you go about interpreting the material you've been given. You're free to experiment, try out new concepts and ideas, and push the boundaries of your thinking to new and unexpected places.

Whatever topic and discipline you're studying, the University's library will be an excellent place for you to start looking for answers. It is crammed full of credible and relevant resources that have already been organised and catalogued for ease of reference, and all these can be consulted at a moment's notice (providing, of course, that someone hasn't already taken out the last copy of the text you're after). Don't worry if you're not particularly tech-savvy – most academic libraries offer students free tutorials on how to make the most of the library database's search functions and access rights, and there's always a member of staff around if you need a bit of extra help.

As well as the University libraries, you will of course have access on site (and most likely at home) to the most expansive resource of all: the Internet. There are multitudes of free essays, journal articles, reports, credible websites, and so on available online – if anything, there's too much! – and using them can save you a fortune on additional textbooks and paid downloads. However, make sure that you verify the authenticity and credibility of any information gathered from a non-academic source such as

Wikipedia, as often these can be misinformed and inaccurately represent the topic you are researching… and never, *ever* reference a Wikipedia article in a bibliography – lecturers, as a rule, do not look kindly upon it.

Despite these resources, you will inevitably end up having to purchase your own copies of some of the more important academic books on your course. That's because you'll need them to hand for several sessions, and will be required to bring them to your classes – the University libraries tend to place strict limits on how long you can keep books for, because they are a shared resource and are meant for everyone's use rather than just yours, so using them in this way isn't really an option. For me, this was no problem – I appreciate any opportunity to invest in a few more books – but many people struggle to both fund and store their academic materials. In terms of storage, I would say that if finding room for bookshelves is a problem for you, or you just don't want to have to lug around a bagful of books every day, investing in a digital reading device such as a Kindle© would be a wise move. These devices are small enough and light enough that you could easily carry your entire digital library around in your pocket. You'll also have a digital back-up if your device ever gets lost.

However, it's worth noting that if you do invest in a large number of paper volumes which you don't really want to hang onto after your studies, many Universities offer a 'buy-back' scheme wherein you can sell your books to the University bookshop for a reasonable price once you've finished with them. This can be a great way to raise funds at the end of your third year if you're a little short of cash: bear in mind, though, that they offer a much lower rate for marked books (which is another good reason not to write in your books!)

Hopefully, this chapter will have given you a better idea of what to expect from your first few days; although, of course, every person's experience will be slightly different. The next chapter focuses specifically on one event that stands out on the academic calendar – Freshers' Week.

Surviving Freshers' Week

What do you get if you mix a few thousand teenagers away from home for the first time, a large quantity of alcohol, a bunch of fancy dress costumes, and a general lack of responsibility? Why, you get Freshers' Week, of course. Freshers' Week is notorious for its supposedly hilarious booze-fuelled antics – and for good reason, too. Some sources have reported that up to one third of all first-year students in the UK suffer an alcohol-related injury within this hectic period, and that many consume in excess of 25 units of alcohol in this first week alone. Now, I don't want to be a spoilsport, but it's no secret that as you get older, you become less able to process large quantities of alcohol. This means that if you partake in Freshers' Week festivities, you need to remain vigilant about how much, and how often, you're drinking.

This might seem an obvious point to make, but University can put a lot of pressure on you – especially if, as an older student, you feel you have something to prove – to be the brightest, funniest and most interesting person in the room. During Freshers' Week, the mother of all icebreakers, you will be meeting a lot of new people, and some of them will have distinctly different ideas to you about what constitutes 'fun'. For instance, on my own Freshers' Week, I encountered a group of around ten or so people, mainly girls, who had thought it a brilliant idea to chain their hands and feet together before embarking on a pub crawl that night. The result was laughable. Having left the keys at home, they were unable to detach themselves to get through doorways, enter toilet cubicles, or generally manoeuvre around a busy city centre without clothes-lining a few people. I later found out that they had spent the night on the steps of the market square: it turned out no one knew how to get back to campus after the University buses had stopped running (as they were all new to the city), and there was no way they could all fit into a mini-cab. All in all, I think it's fair to say that they did *not* have a good night out.

So, let's get one thing straight right now: there's nothing wrong with having a laugh and getting involved (or even having a few drinks and letting your hair down), but just remember that you don't have to be a teenager to succumb to peer pressure. Avoid emulating your wilder youth and trying to 'get down with the kids' where you can. For example, don't try and keep up in the drinking games if the most you're used to is a glass of chardonnay at dinner – before you know it there'll be incriminating evidence all over Facebook of your drunken exploits, and no one wants to be the butt of a joke. Admittedly, sometimes this can be hard to avoid without avoiding socialisation completely: most of the Freshers' Week culture is based around the consumption of alcohol – they even make T-shirts to celebrate how much you've managed to drink! –but when it comes down to it, it's *you* who is going to have to wake up to that hangover, so don't be afraid to say that enough's enough and make your way home whilst you can still remember where exactly that is!

If you get so drunk that you don't know what's happening, you don't really need me to point out the obvious (although I'm going to anyway): you're potentially putting yourself in danger of having an accident, which could lead to quite serious injuries (which is the last thing you need in the first week of your studies), and you are also potentially making yourself more vulnerable in the eyes of other people.

Now please don't get me wrong… I'm certainly not saying that people who are taken advantage of whilst drunk are to blame for what happens – far from it! However, each year local police warn new students that thieves and criminals hone in on 'soft targets' (that is, people who might not be as acutely aware of themselves, their surroundings and their belongings as the average person), and by becoming so inebriated that you're not sure what's happening, you are potentially placing yourself in this category. Just make sure that when you're out having a good time, both you and your belongings are safe.

Another important point to make is that you shouldn't feel pressurised into attending every single event, club night, meet-up, games day or icebreaker that's offered. Not only is it a brutal schedule, but it also leaves you very little time to pursue any interests or hobbies that you will sustain throughout your academic life. There are a multitude of clubs, societies and teams that you can join – some fun, some sporty, and some that are just plain stupid (the Biscuit Appreciation Society springs to mind) – and this offers a vital opportunity early on for you to make friends with common interests. I, for example, joined a Literary Appreciation Society, the Nature Preservation Society, and RocSoc (The Rock Music Appreciation Society), as well as signing up for information on music events, poetry recitals and art exhibitions that were of interest to me when I studied at NTU. However, I know people who signed up for *everything* and found themselves only able to make one meeting in every four or five (as they were spread so thinly), meaning they never really got settled in any one group.

There are only a few events during Freshers' Week that you *have* to attend – these will include a general orientation assembly (which mostly involves listening to a series of long and increasingly boring speeches about what to do and what not to do at University) and the registration process (which is where you confirm that you're here and ready to learn, get your official timetable for classes, and pose for your photo ID card).

So, what I'm trying to say is this: try not to get overwhelmed. You don't have to determine your entire academic social life in the very first week, and as your studies progress, you may find yourself developing new interests and hobbies. There's no hurry to sign up for everything that's on offer – in fact, quality in your choices matters far more than quantity during Freshers' Week. Try and find at least one club which appeals to your current hobbies and habits, and at least one that offers you an opportunity to do something you've always wanted to, but never had the opportunity before. It doesn't matter if it's pole-dancing, nature preservation, snowboarding, mural painting, boxing, or political activism – there'll be a club for it!

You'll soon be meeting a variety of interesting people in addition to the people you'll see very day in your classes, and making connections with people you never would have imagined yourself being friends with. That's one of the best things about University – the people you meet will teach you things you could never learn in a classroom, and all you have to do to learn something new is to turn and speak to the person sitting next to you.

Hopefully, this chapter will have given you an idea of what you can expect from Freshers' Week, and the pitfalls to avoid if you want to enjoy the festivities. The next chapter concerns itself with how to make friends in unexpected places.

Making Friends in Unexpected Places

I place a lot of importance in this book upon making friends at University, and there's a good reason why. It's not just about finding a buddy to go drinking with, or to share the dirt with on your fellow classmates (although both of those things can be fun). At the end of the day, you've chosen to attend University to gain a *qualification*, and because it could potentially open doors for you in the future. Believe it or not, your peers actually form a vital part of this equation.

Making friends at University can actually enhance your experience of learning in a number of different ways: they can offer you support with your studies, share their knowledge with you, and provide you with constructive feedback on your creative ideas. Furthermore, once University's over, you might find you have a few friends in the right places – whether that means they are working in a company you'd like to join, or just happen to know people who might be able to give you a leg-up into your career of choice. For the moment, though, let's focus on the advantages whilst you're still attending University.

Out of everybody in your life, your fellow students are probably the ones who best understand the current difficulties and challenges you face. You are probably already painfully aware that in most facets of society, students have been labelled as being "lazy" and "riotous", and you may thus feel unable to discuss the issues you're facing with someone who doesn't know what it's like to undertake such an intense period of learning. Many people just don't understand that a lot of students get up at midday because they stayed up all night doing their assigned reading or finishing an essay, or that booze-fuelled nights out are just their way of "playing hard". In this regard, simply being able to discuss your worries, stresses and frustrations with your peers can provide you with crucial pressure relief when you need it most.

In some cases, they are also familiar with the topic you are studying, because they're on the same course or studying a similar discipline. Some of the closest friends I had at University were on the same course as me; our friendships developed naturally, as we all spent time together before, during and after classes. I knew that they were studying the same material as I was, and I respected their opinions even when we disagreed about the meaning of a text or its importance – in fact, disagreements were particularly helpful, as they helped me to see things from another perspective and further enhance my understanding. They are, therefore, a vital resource which you can utilise to ensure you get the most out of yourself and your degree.

Taking advantage of this resource is really quite easy. I would thoroughly recommend that you invest time developing an academic support system wherein you and your classmates can get together frequently to discuss ideas from your classes, the issues you're having, and any tips any of you have for making the student life a little easier. All this really takes initially is the agreement to do so: you can meet in an informal environment, perhaps once a week, and see where each session takes you. Once you gain a better idea of the needs of the group, you can then start to tailor the focus of sessions and make sure that they are of benefit to everybody. In my third year, I found these impromptu workshop sessions invaluable; because I had already had the opportunity to 'test' my ideas, I felt much more confident going into classes where I would be expected to express my ideas to the group, and so was a lot more likely to participate in group discussions. This, of course, can only be beneficial in terms of your education.

OK, so I've covered some of the reasons *why* you should make friends, but I haven't really addressed *how* to do so up until now. As a mature student, the idea of going back to school and having to start all over again can be scary (especially if you didn't have all that great a time of it first time round). However, you don't need to worry: making friends at University can actually be very easy. There are a few things you should bear in mind, though.

Firstly, just as you can't judge a book by its cover, neither can you ascertain a person's intelligence and/or likeability through observation of their acid green nails and matching hairdo. At University, people will inevitably surprise you. Those who, at first glance, seem alien to you may end up sharing the same thought patterns and mental processes. One of my closest classroom allies, for example, looked as if she had fallen from the pages of *Cosmopolitan*; we couldn't have been more different. She was the sort of person I would have avoided as a teenager, and certainly wouldn't have pictured us ever being friends. However, when it came down to it, we almost always agreed when it came to academic opinions. I guess what I'm saying is that, sometimes, similar minds can lurk in the strangest of places. Don't pass up the opportunity to get to know someone based on assumptions (whether about their beliefs, accent or fashion sense) or you may be missing out – like I might have done the first time round.

Also, don't rule out a potential friend purely because they're younger than you. Given that you will be older than most of the people at your University (bar the staff), it's really not a good idea to rule these people out. I'm not saying that you shouldn't make friends with the other mature students you meet – in fact, I would actively encourage it – but don't assume that someone will be immature because they're younger. Age is, after all, just a number! Younger students will (of course) have encountered adults before and won't be intimidated by your age, but they might not be used to being treated as an adult, and so you may find that your friendship offers them a refreshing and welcome change of attitude.

At University, I was the oldest member of my core group of friends – in fact, at times it became a bit of a running joke. What I soon realised during my own experiences at University was that unless you start threatening to clean their room, most of the younger students you meet will probably just be pleased to have someone around with a little life experience under their belt who treats them as an equal. Be warned, though: if you violate these terms of equality by trying to pass along all your years of wisdom, you may find yourself frustrated. Just as you had to learn from your own mistakes, so do your younger counterparts. Lectures about drinking too much/staying out/sleeping around/wasting money should be avoided (for no other reason than you'd be wasting your breath) – let their mothers worry about that!

Hopefully, this chapter will have given you a few ideas of ways you could meet new people – and hopefully make a few friends! – at University. The next chapter will consider how to cope when the demands of your course begin to feel overwhelming.

Tackling Your Subject Head-On

At some point during your studies, you may find yourself questioning why on Earth you picked this subject: other people seem to be having an easier time of it, whilst you feel completely overwhelmed by the sheer amount of knowledge you are expected to have. I can assure you that it's a feeling that almost every student experiences, even when the subject they've chosen is all they've ever imagined or wanted to study.

Take me, for instance. I fell in love with the magical art of storytelling from an early age and haven't had my head out of a book since, and so my choice of subject at University was a simple one. Though I have numerous interests, I couldn't imagine studying anything other than English Literature and Creative Writing when it came to filling in that UCAS form. Nor do I regret my decision, now that it's all over – I think it's important to point that out from the outset. It was a tough journey, but I honestly wouldn't trade it for anything. However, there were times when I was ready to throw in the towel. In order to give you an idea of why, I'm going to share with you my own experiences of the challenges that any student faces.

Firstly, let me explain how studying made my greatest love the source of most of the stress in my student life. I'm talking, of course, about books. Although, at first, the idea of lining my shelves with dozens of new volumes filled me with absolute glee, my love of reading was tested to the absolute limit during my Bachelor's degree. Booklists became both my instructors and my nemesis: I felt like I was constantly battling with myself to read as much as I could, as fast as I could, and absorb it all. Please, don't get me wrong here – some of the assigned texts were an absolute joy to read, and a couple even changed my life. I will never forget the first time I encountered William Blake, for example, or the intense reactions I had to reading African fiction written by the likes of J.M. Coetzee, Chinua Achebe and Achmat Dangor. Texts that I considered familiar, such as Bram Stoker's *Dracula* or Kurt Vonnegut's *Cat's Cradle*, were transformed into something new, something different, something which conveyed a message that I had never noticed before. Even some of the texts and writers I found challenging (James Joyce springs to mind) have taught me something fundamental about that which I love most – the art of storytelling. However, that can't be said for *every* book. The truth is that you may find yourself reading nothing but the indecipherable, the bewildering, or the painfully dull for weeks on end.

Another factor to consider is the actual *amount* you have to read at any given time. At one point, I was crunching through more than five books, plus additional essays, every week – a blistering pace for anyone to keep up. However, you *do* have to keep it up… a degree is an endurance race, and trust me, it will require all of your stamina. My advice? *Keep on top of your reading.* Even better, try to get ahead of the game. It may seem like I'm stating the obvious, but the set reading for classes has a way of sneaking up on you when deadlines are looming, and when you've done a hard day's graft, it's all too easy to put off. Ignore it at your peril. Even a slack week or two will leave a pile of backdated work big enough to send the most dedicated bookworm away screaming! This only intensifies as you progress through to your third year of study, and so it's a good idea to get yourself into good habits and positive routines in regards to your reading habits from the very start of your course. I used to plan out the time to read each book I had to study on a week-by-week basis, so that I never got caught out by an unexpected assignment. Even then, though, I found that sometimes it was a real challenge to stay motivated to finish my night's reading before letting myself clock off and relax – sometimes you're really not going to be in the mood for studying, but these are the moments when you'll really need to get yourself motivated, because the longer you put it off, the less likely you are to get around to doing it. Just as in work, if you don't do your bit you won't get paid, if you don't put in the time and effort with your studies, you won't get the grades you want and deserve.

So, what I'm really saying is that the only thing you can do is get your head down, hang in there and keep at it. Just keep reminding yourself that you're learning all this for a reason, and that there's a light at the end of the tunnel (albeit one that's very far away). Also, as silly as it sounds, introducing a reward system can actually help you keep up the pace. I would recommend that you try customising your treats so that it's something you can really look forward to… for me, it was cigarettes, Coca-Cola and Jammie Dodgers (not the healthiest variation, I know, but it certainly did the trick!)

At this point, I think it's also important to point out something else that may surprise you: there *is* such a thing as reading *too much*. There are more studies, critiques, reviews, books, journal articles and essays available out there than one person could possibly read, and critics rarely tend to agree. Trying to incorporate all those opinions into your work only serves to muddle your ideas. Moreover, trying to read it all tends to turn you into a crazy person. From experience, I would say choose quality over quantity when selecting secondary reading material. You will certainly not be expected to read *every* book that's available on your subject, but your lecturers will expect you to root out the good ones. You will have already been supplied with a list of viable options in your course materials, so this is a good place to start – after all, it's better that you spend a decent amount of time studying the books that really matter, rather than spreading yourself so thinly that you can't really recall anything you've read. If need be, you can purchase academic breakdowns of any difficult texts you encounter and study them carefully. This can be very helpful when you're studying something you simply don't understand, or where the language used makes ideas difficult to decipher. At the end of the day though, your lecturers will want to see your *own* interpretations of what you've been given, rather than you simply regurgitating the opinions of other critics. Show that you understand the intricacies of what you're studying and you will be rewarded. Trust me – my highest marks (significantly high firsts) were earned this way!

Hopefully, this chapter will have provided you with the sense that you are not alone, if nothing else. The truth is that everyone feels the pressure at some point, but you've just got to hang in there! The next chapter will look at some of the ways you can stop your home life interfering with your studies.

Ensuring Life Doesn't Get in the Way

Picture this: you have your assigned reading pinned open at the appropriate page whilst also trying to cook dinner for the family, but you've been re-reading the same paragraph for the last ten minutes because the kids keep interrupting, and they're charging about, playing, running around your feet. Although you'd love to indulge them, you've got a big assignment due in a few days and you're behind, so instead you keep trying to do twenty things at once… eventually, you burn the dinner, fall out with the kids, and can't remember a word from the book you've been trying to get to all evening.

Sound familiar? Even if you don't have children (and/or don't do the cooking), this passage still probably has a ring of truth about it. That's because attending University whilst trying to maintain the usual state of domestic normality can make you feel a bit like you're leading a double life. Though this is something all students experience to some degree, for those who have external responsibilities – such as the upkeep of the home, the paying of bills, a part-time job, or perhaps a family, partner and/or family member to care for – the pressure can be pretty daunting. Many mature students find themselves constantly having to juggle their work, home and school lives as result of their increased workload; having to meet the demands of each of these areas, and never really getting any time off for a rest.

If this sounds like you, then I need to point out that spreading yourself this thinly can have not only a profoundly negative impact upon your schoolwork, but also upon your physical and mental health. Prolonged stress is linked to a myriad of health issues, including problems with concentration, insomnia, anxiety disorders and panic attacks, depression, increased blood pressure, higher levels of cholesterol in the body, a weaker immune system, lower bone density, nausea, and stomach cramping. It can even increase period pain for women and lower sperm count in men… and that list is just scratching the surface of the potential negative effects of remaining stressed over long periods of time. For instance, it doesn't exactly improve familial and personal relations – no one likes getting their head bitten off all the time by someone who is constantly irritable, and because (as noted in the previous chapter) non-students often believe studying at University is an 'easy ride', genuine demonstrations of stress and an inability to cope with it often end up being ignored or misinterpreted.

Of course, these aspects of your world are bound to clash from time to time, particularly if you're trying to do your academic work in the family home, but what should you do about it? You certainly can't be expected to spend all of your study time behaving as if you don't have any other responsibilities, and your home time ignoring your studies (and your worries about them). It just wouldn't work! That's because you are so much more than *just* a student, mother, father, sister, worker, carer, or friend. You're a multi-faceted and multi-talented human being, and as a result, you *can* be all of these things at once. However, it can be tough being this talented. Sometimes it's okay to take a little time out from your other roles to focus on something that's important to you – like your studies.

Be honest with your friends and family – let them know that you need time and space away from them to concentrate on your studies, because attaining this qualification is really important to you. If they love you, they'll give you what you need (even if they don't really understand why you need it). This is especially important if you do a lot of your schoolwork at home, and there are often other people around. Assign yourself a workspace free of crayons, water bills, ironing and shopping lists (ideally, with a door you can close behind you when you need some peace and quiet!) and make sure you clear your mind of all the other, non-University related things you need to think about. After all, concentration is the key to success!

It doesn't matter how you go about creating this work space – if it means converting the spare room into your own private study, then go for it. If you have a dining room but everyone eats their dinner from trays in the lounge, put that table top to good use and use it as a desk. If the only quiet spot you can think of is the garden, try setting yourself up in the shed with a desk, a lamp and a comfy old chair – as long as it's somewhere relatively comfortable and quiet, and you can see what you're doing, it doesn't matter where you go to study. If this really isn't an option for you, consider taking advantage of the late-night library opening hours – very few people are around at that time of night, and if you're able to access these facilities with relative ease, it can be a wonderfully serene place to collect your thoughts.

Also, try to set time aside each week specifically to complete any outstanding assignments for coursework or classes. This can be difficult, but without set working hours, it's all too easy to put things off. If you're struggling to find free time, try putting together a timetable which details when you're at University, when you're at home but need to be focused on your studying, when you've got time to kick back and relax. This can be particularly effective if you are juggling a family life along with your studies, as it gives everyone around you a clear idea of when you're not to be disturbed. However, you may find that you have to sacrifice your 'weekend break': one of the challenges of being a student is that you have to cater your working schedule to your deadlines, rather than being able to study when you get the time.

Another odd thing about studying at University as a mature student is that whilst sometimes it will feel like everything is happening at once, at other times you will be stuck waiting around for hours on end. Classes will be spaced over the course of a week, so you may find that you have some days with no classes at all, some days that are jam-packed, and other days where you will have several hours to burn in between when your classes start. I won't lie – it can be frustrating, especially once you've gotten into the habit of the working day being 9am-5pm. If you know you're gong to be stuck hanging around on certain days, it's a good idea to get into the habit of bringing work with you and using your free time to study. It's very easy to spend your spare four or so hours chatting over drinks in the Student Union instead of studying – I'm guilty of that myself! – but when you do eventually get home, that big old pile of work is still going to be there, waiting for you. So, the more you manage to get done in your 'in-between' time, the more likely you are to get all your assignments up to date… and there's no greater feeling than knowing you can chill out and do whatever you like, guilt-free, because all your work is done!

Hopefully, this chapter will have given you a few helpful hints regarding how to keep your home life relatively separate from your work life. The next chapter discusses how to cope when it comes round to your final exams.

Coping with Exam Stress

This section is dedicated to the summer event that pretty much every University student dreads – the examination period. Although you may have taken exams before, and may even have done well, there's nothing quite as intense or intimidating (that I've experienced, anyway) as doing it at University level. It's a time when even the strongest student can crumble under the sheer pressure of it all. Not only are the questions lot harder, and the expectation for an in-depth answer much higher, but the stakes are higher, too. Unless you've got a very good reason for not passing first time round, any retakes will usually be capped at 40% - this means that you cannot attain anything higher than a borderline pass for that exam if it's retaken, even if you aced it the second time round.

Subsequently, there is a huge amount of pressure on everyone taking their summer examinations to get it right first time… and when you have absolutely no idea what's going to come up as a question, that means having to be prepared for pretty much anything! Students are expected to remember huge quantities of data (whether that's mathematical formulae, or literary quotes – no subject really gets a break in this regard) and be able to recall and apply it to any scenario. No matter what, you're expected to keep your cool, think the question through, and give the best answer you can.

That's an awful lot for any one person to pull off, no matter how academically gifted or determined they are. However, there are things that you can do to give yourself the best possible chance of performing well on the day. This chapter will discuss a few of these, offering advice that will hopefully help you to overcome your nerves, get on top of your revision, and be prepared when you do sit down to take these tests.

Well, first things first – one of the best pieces of advice I can give you is to start your exam revision as early as possible. I know they're the last thing you'll want to be thinking about in the spring, but the truth is that all too many people leave it too late… they begin studying a couple of weeks beforehand, and then wonder why they feel completely unprepared when the big day comes. Don't let yourself be blindsighted! The earlier you begin your revision, the more prepared you'll be, as you'll have given your brain plenty of time to properly process and absorb all the information you're trying to remember. This, in turn, will make the accessing and recalling of this information much easier during your actual exam. Plus, having confidence in the fact that you know your stuff means that exam nerves are bound to be reduced – this is a real bonus, when everyone around you seems to be losing their head! Admittedly, in the final year, this can be more difficult to pull off, as dissertation deadlines usually fall in late April or May – however, you can complete both your dissertation and your revision at once and still give both sufficient focus, if you plan for it correctly.

That leads me nicely onto my next point. Once you've decided to commit to your revision, I would recommend drawing up some form of plan detailing all the topic areas you need to study for each exam, along with a timetable of when you'll be able to focus on each of them. Plan this timetable around when your exams will actually come up – don't prepare for the final exam first, and leave the first exam's revision to the last minute, or plan to revise for something after the exam has already passed. Sounds boring and neurotic, I know, but it's amazing how breaking your revision up into little bite-size chunks can make it a lot less intimidating overall.

However, make sure that when you're planning your time, you allow for adequate breaks and rest time. This may seem like a lot to ask, especially given the time management issues discussed in the previous chapter, but it is essential that during a stressful period, you allow yourself to cool off a bit. You are not a machine, and you can't expect your brain to suddenly start performing like one! The average person's concentration span is between 40-50 minutes, so bear this is mind when creating your timetable. A good method is to segment your time into hours, allowing for a 10 minute break at the end of each time period, before you move onto something else.

Another thing to note at this point is that studying for excessively long periods at a time is not necessarily the best way to go about your revision. I know a lot of people thinking 'cramming' is effective (and at lower levels, it sometimes can be), but there's simply too much to remember at University level for this technique to really work. Sessions that last more than six hours are bound to be a waste of your time, because your brain cannot continue to perform at optimum levels for such long periods. A lot of what you revise simply won't be absorbed, and you'll find yourself having to go over it again and again – something which is as time-consuming as it is frustrating.

Just like a long-distance runner, you will need to figure out your own optimal performance times, and use this to your advantage. That's because exam revision, like your degree as a whole, is not a sprint – it's an endurance race. You can't go pedal-to-the-metal all the time, but if you identify the times that you're at your peak and use this time to study, you'll find that the overall amount of time you need to spend studying will decrease, but that you remember a lot more of what you've revised and can recall it more easily. Some people are better first thing in the morning, before the day's had time to interrupt them, but for me, it was the evenings… my mind always seemed sharper after a certain time of night, and so I would use this time to get the lion's share of my studying and revision done.

Even with provisions like these in place, it's still all too easy to let exam nerves get the better of you. If you're feeling this way, you're certainly not alone – according to surveys conducted by the National Union of Students, only 2% of all University students reported that they experienced little to no stress during this period. As noted in the previous chapter, stress can have all sorts of negative effects on your health, your energy levels, and your ability to concentrate. The best advice I can give you, then, is to not isolate yourself and go through it alone. It doesn't help to bottle up feelings of helplessness, anxiety or outright panic, and no one will think you're weak for admitting that you're having a tough time of it. Talk to your classmates, your family and friends, or even the stranger sitting next to you at the bus stop on your way home – whatever you are most comfortable with.

Your classmates are, as noted in Chapter 4 ('Making Friends in Unexpected Places'), one of the best resources available to you when it comes to getting advice, sharing your fears, or generally just letting off a bit of steam about how frustrated you are. Don't be afraid to ask for their help and advice: if you've set up a study group, make sure that when it's getting closer to exams, you all meet up regularly (even if it's just for a chat). You're surrounded by people who know what you're going through, so there's no need to suffer in silence.

If you're struggling and/or falling behind and really don't feel comfortable asking your fellow classmates, then approach your lecturers directly. They are, after all, there to help you! Moreover, you'll find that their feedback and assistance can be a valuable resource when negotiating the academic minefield: they will know all the complexities of the material you are studying, and will have studied it themselves in great detail. Most professors and lecturers will make themselves available for drop-in chats at certain times of the day, and so familiarise yourself with when their doors will be 'open' to you and make sure you take advantage of the opportunity they're offering! In addition, there are also external support networks available, which you can find out about by asking a representative of your local Student's Union. This can be especially useful if you haven't got a study group set up, or you're unable to meet up with them regularly because of prior commitments.

All of this planning and preparation all inevitably boils down to how you're doing on the day though, of course. There are a few things that you can do to ensure you're in good form when it comes to sitting down to take the exam itself. Firstly, stay hydrated – an obvious point, but something that is often overlooked in the fidgety, nervous build-up to an exam. It's a proven medical fact that your ability to perform well will be hindered by being dehydrated, and you can't exactly pop out for a cuppa half-way through. Make sure you take a bottle of water in with you in addition to any soft or hot drinks.

Secondly – another obvious point – make sure that your mobile phone is switched off (take the battery out if you have one of those phones that will switch itself on for certain things, such as alarms) and that you're not carrying any exam notes in with you. This is considered a serious offence, as it indicates a desire to cheat. I know people that have done this without thinking, with devastating consequences. Make sure to take a moment before you go inside to check that you're carrying everything you need (pen, water bottle, calculator/other instruments if needed), and that you've put everything else away in your bag.

Thirdly, a neat little trick: exactly thirty minutes before the exam starts, eat something, like an apple or a chocolate bar. This ensures that you will get a boost of energy at the exact right time – just as you're turning over the question paper – and will help with your general levels of concentration, energy and memory recall ability.

Finally, don't forget to *breathe.* It's very easy to let yourself slip into 'panic mode' and to subsequently throw yourself at the exam paper without any sort of consideration or prior planning. In a lot of subjects, you will be expected to write your answers in essay form, and taking a moment or two to think about exactly how you're going to answer the question can ensure that you produce a better organised and more focused piece of work overall. If it helps, use the first page of your answer booklet to draw out a brief essay plan – there aren't any rules against this, and in some institutions, it's actively encouraged. You can even allocate yourself time for each section of the essay, ensuring you don't get caught out by the clock. This is great, because it means you're never stuck having to try and scribble all of your thoughts down in a few measly minutes at the end.

Hopefully, this chapter has given you a better idea of how to cope with taking your end-of-year examinations, and how to prepare for them in such a way as to ensure low levels of stress, and high levels of success! The next chapter considers what you should do once you've got your qualification.

Deciding What to Do Once It's All Over

During my third year, my friends and I would often joke about what a relief it would be to graduate from University. We fantasised about escaping the pressure of deadlines, being judged on something other than grade percentages, and reading books we actually liked for a change. What I was not prepared for was the overwhelming feeling of sadness I felt once it was all over, knowing that I wouldn't be going back that autumn. I know what you're thinking – the grass is always greener, and all that. You may even have a point. However, the truth is that I still miss studying at University, even now. I had a reason to broach new subjects, conduct in-depth research, and to stretch myself to the limit comprehending complex ideas. In fact, that's part of the reason that I am in my current line of work – it has often been compared to "studying for a living", which makes me very happy indeed.

However, I would be lying if I said it had been easy to get to where I am now. Unfortunately, graduating with a decent degree won't necessarily guarantee that you will be able to get the job of your dreams straight away. If you've decided to pursue studies in an area in which you already have professional experience (such as nursing, social care or management), you will undoubtedly have an advantage over some of your younger, more inexperienced peers, but even then, the hard work is far from over (unless, of course, you are lucky enough to already have a job lined up waiting for you!). Many mature graduates are finding that competition in the working world is greater than ever, and that a decent degree plus experience doesn't necessarily guarantee you work.

If job applications have you feeling like you're swimming against the proverbial tide, never fear! If you're smart, there *are* ways to distinguish yourself from the masses. However, there are a few things you're going to need in order to get ahead. The first – and most important – characteristic you will need is *patience*. Even though you're eager to show off your newly-acquired skills in a brand new job, it's worth noting that few people manage to secure something right away. That doesn't mean that your perfect job isn't out there – just that you might have to wait a little while for it. Even if you *do* get accepted onto a company's graduate scheme, be prepared for quite a lengthy application process. Many companies administer numeracy, literacy, accuracy and reasoning tests in addition to forms and CVs to ensure they find the best candidates possible. If the idea of this makes you nervous, practice tests are available free online – I would recommend that you try out a few and see how your skills match up.

In addition to *patience,* you will also need to demonstrate *perseverance* when job-hunting after University. Some students with more generalised degrees (like my own BA in English with Creative Writing) may experience a sinking sensation when they realise that their credentials are not necessarily a VIP pass into a better career. Unfortunately, unless you have undertaken a specialist subject with a definite career in mind, you may find your employment casting-net is wide but full of holes. There *are* employers out there who will require your unique set of skills. However, to find them, you may have to persevere and play the long game. Try to provide yourself with as many reference points as possible. You could, for example, register yourself with all the graduate websites and employment agencies covering your area. Universities, too, often provide career development services and advice for their alumni, and will bend over backwards to help you find work (for if nothing else, it makes their stats look good). LinkedIn, Twitter and Facebook are also great avenues to explore. The majority of companies nowadays are making the most of social media to extend both their client and employment bases, regardless of their size. There's no reason why you can't do the same!

Another important trait you will need to demonstrate post-graduation is *positivity*. Have you ever heard the expression 'first impressions count'? Well, it's never been more relevant than when establishing your career. That's because prospective employers rely upon the candidate's descriptions of their own abilities, and only meet face-to-face with you once they're convinced. If executed correctly, your curriculum vitae is arguably the most powerful weapon in your arsenal – and be assured, the fight to gain employment is a battle royale. You will have limited space available upon CVs and applications to sell yourself, so make each word count. Try to view yourself objectively: what are your strengths and most impressive achievements? What skills and experience did you gain during your time at University? Which of your personal traits compliment the role(s) you are applying for? Bear in mind that even a potential weakness can be viewed as a strength, if it's given the right spin. For example, an individual could be a painstaking perfectionist (which is an example of the negative perspective), or alternatively, they could be determined, accurate and hold themselves to very high standards (which is the more positive perspective).

Whatever industry you're trying to break into, your potential employers will all have one thing in common: they'll want to hire someone who's excited about the job they're offering! That's why, in addition to all these other characteristics, you will need to demonstrate *passion.* Though this may seem like common sense, many people overlook enthusiasm for the role or company entirely and focus on their professional credentials. *Big* mistake! No matter how well qualified you are, it's important to let the company know that you're genuinely interested in the role. Try being proactive and finding out a little about how the business operates. You may find there's more to it than meets the eye, and it never hurts to be well-informed! Having a clearer idea of how you would like to progress within the company shows forward-thinking and a genuine desire to join their fold – and when you're asking someone to invest in your future, passion for their cause is an absolute must.

Finally, like it or not, the time may come when you have to go back to studying of some kind to secure the job you want – that's because *prowess* is also needed if you want to be successful in the employment market. Unless your degree specialises in computing, for example, you may find employers need some form of official certification as evidence of your IT skills. Though you will probably have used some (if not all) of the basic programmes you will need, you need to prove you are able to do so in a professional capacity. This doesn't necessarily mean months of study – many courses (particularly those covering MS Office) are free and can be completed in a matter of hours. However, this isn't always the case, as I've found whilst trying to teach myself how to use Adobe Creative Suite (don't laugh, I know I'm a little behind the times). Sometimes a little more elbow grease is what's required… and after all the hard work you've already put in, what's a little more?

Hopefully, you will now have gained a better understanding of some of the ways you can help yourself to get the job of your dreams after graduation. Don't be afraid to tell everyone how talented you are, and how much you want the job, and most importantly of all, *don't give up!*

Conclusion

We've now reached the end of the book. I hope that the hints, tips, anecdotes and advice contained in these chapters have helped to give you a better idea of what to expect as a mature student going to University – whether that be during the application process, throughout your studies, or once it's all over and done with, and you've got your degree.

Although I can only provide you with my own subjective experience, I do think that certain aspects of University life are the same, no matter who you are or what you're studying. All students are united in purpose, in action, and in their intended destination: academic success. Age doesn't change that… although, I've found that those who have already been through a few of life's trials are all the more determined to face whatever's coming. Even as part of the alumni, you're always connected to your University, your classmates, and to students as a whole, because you've all travelled that same road, faced the same challenges, and have ultimately come out the other side with something to be proud of.

The last piece of advice I'll offer you is this: don't ever lose your grit, determination, and pride in what you're doing.

That's what got you here in the first place, and it's what will carry you over the finish line – never let yourself forget that! Obtaining that qualification may not be easy, but it's worth the effort. Keep reminding yourself why you're there, what you have set out to achieve, and how far you've come already. There's nothing wrong with giving yourself a pat on the back every now and then, and this undertaking gives you good reason to hold your head high! A lot of people in your shoes would have chosen the easy route, but you've had the guts and determination to go for what you really wanted.

Finally, before I leave you, I'd like to wish you the best of luck in your studies. I hope that you attain whatever qualification it is that you've set out to achieve, and that you are able to use it to bring about the changes in your life that you envisioned when you applied.

Stay strong, keep believing in yourself, and don't ever take your eye off the prize. See you on the other side!

- **Joanne M. Weselby**

August 2014

About Joanne M. Weselby

Joanne M. Weselby (1985-) was born in Sutton in Ashfield, England and grew up a stone's throw from Sherwood Forest.

As an adult, she went on to obtain a first class BA (Hons) in English Literature and Creative Writing from Nottingham Trent University in 2012, and was awarded both the Five Leaves Prize and the Pat McLernon Prize for outstanding academic achievements in her chosen field.

She now works freelance as a writer, academic researcher and copyeditor.

Books by Joanne M. Weselby

- 'First Class English Essays: A Collection of Short Essays'
- 'Citations Made Simple: A Guide to Easy Referencing'
- 'Never Too Late: A Mature Student's Guide to Going to University'

Success Stories?

If, after reading this book, you've found it to be helpful, why not let myself and others know about it by posting a review?

Alternatively, visit my Fan Page on Facebook at:
https://www.facebook.com/jmweselby
Like, share, and leave me a comment –
I'd be delighted to hear from you!

7425180R00038

Printed in Great Britain
by Amazon.co.uk, Ltd.,
Marston Gate.